This is a tiger salamander. Tiger salamanders are amphibians, like toads and frogs. Amphibians can live on land and in water. They hatch from eggs in ponds or streams.

Tiger salamanders are about 3 to 6 inches long. Some can grow to 13 inches. Their skin is thin, moist, and slippery. They don't have claws.

# Tiger Salamander's Amazing Tail

## By Katacha Díaz

**Scott Foresman**
is an imprint of

Glenview, Illinois • Boston, Massachusetts • Chandler, Arizona •
Upper Saddle River, New Jersey

**Photographs**

Every effort has been made to secure permission and provide appropriate credit for photographic material. The publisher deeply regrets any omission and pledges to correct errors called to its attention in subsequent editions.

Unless otherwise acknowledged, all photographs are the property of Pearson Education, Inc.

Photo locators denoted as follows: Top (T), Center (C), Bottom (B), Left (L), Right (R), Background (Bkgd)

**Opener:** ©David M Dennis/Oxford Scientific/PhotoLibrary Group, Inc.; **1** ©Geoff Brightling/©DK Images; **3** ©Chris Mattison/Alamy Images; **4** ©David M Dennis/Oxford Scientific/PhotoLibrary Group, Inc.; **5** (L) ©Jerry Young/©DK Images, (R) ©Geoff Brightling/©DK Images; **6** ©Peter Arnold, Inc./Alamy Images; **7** ©Mary Clay/Ardea; **8** ©Leszczynski, Zigmund/Animals Animals/Earth Scenes; **9** (BL) ©FogStock/Index Open, (TL, R) Photos to Go/Photolibrary; **10** Photos to Go/Photolibrary; **11** ©Robert Shantz/Alamy Images; **12** Spectrum Photofile.

ISBN 13: 978-0-328-46918-5
ISBN 10:     0-328-46918-1

3 4 5 6 7 8 9 10 V010 13 12 11 10

Chameleon
lizard

Tiger
salamander

How are these two animals the same?
How are they different? Lizards have ears
and dry scaly skin. They also have claws.
Lizards are reptiles, not amphibians.

Tiger salamanders need water to live. They breathe and drink water through their skin. So they make their homes near ponds, streams, or rain puddles.

Tiger salamanders are very good hunters. They eat tadpoles, snails, and small fish. They also like to eat insects, mice, and worms.

Tiger salamanders are small, so they have lots of enemies. They find homes that are safe. You might find one under a rock or a log. Some live in holes under the ground.

Who likes to eat tiger salamanders?
They make a tasty treat for owls, snakes,
and coyotes.

But Mother Nature gave the tiger salamander a special gift. There's poison in its tail! First it warns its enemies. It lifts its head and its tail.

Some enemies take the hint and go away. But one might try to grab the tiger salamander's tail. When that happens, the tail comes off! Milky poison shoots out, and the tiger salamander escapes!

The tiger salamander might not have a tail now, but guess what? It grows a new one!

Isn't that amazing?